Charles H. Gabriel

Sunshine

songs for Sunday schools

Charles H. Gabriel

Sunshine
songs for Sunday schools

ISBN/EAN: 9783337265397

Printed in Europe, USA, Canada, Australia, Japan

Cover: Foto ©Lupo / pixelio.de

More available books at **www.hansebooks.com**

SUNSHINE

Songs for

SUNDAY SCHOOLS

BY

CHAS. H. GABRIEL

AUTHOR OF

Salvation Songs, Vineyard Songs, Scripture Songs, Songs of the Pentecost, Gospel and Temperance Songs, Epworth Songs, Little Branches, Songs for the Harvest Field, Gabriel's Sunday School Songs, etc.

COPYRIGHT, 1895, BY MEYER & BROTHER

PUBLISHED BY
MEYER & BROTHER
108 Washington Street
CHICAGO, ILL.

PREFACE.

A song is the expression of some phase of the heart's emotion, and, as the heart aspires to better things, so the song should enlarge all these feelings, in their different lights and shadows: songs of gratitude, gladness, thanksgiving and praise; songs aspiring to higher levels in heart-life, teaching great Scripture truths; songs that are prayers for the heart's longing, etc., etc., should be abundantly supplied and sung in a full knowledge and spirit of the sentiment expressed; the words may be read and properly emphasized before singing.

A song may be known and liked in one school, and yet be unappreciated in another:—select only such as are in favor with the singers; do not insist upon the use of an unpopular piece simply because it is appropriate to the lesson. Sing often! sing at least one new song each session; sing the popular songs frequently, that the hymn may become fixed in the memory; a song, well committed and rightly sung, is more to be desired than a lesson carelessly prepared and indifferently taught.

The success of music in the Sunday School depends largely upon the class of songs used, and the manner of their using.

THE SONG should be one of sunshine and praise. When occasion demands seriousness, sing a hymn from memory, to one of the grand old Church tunes, which should, in every Sunday School, be taught the children, that they may at all sessions of worship "Sing with the spirit and with the understanding."

THE LEADER must possess special ability, and carry into the work right method, wise judgment and prompt action, and must be a person who can make of the song a beautiful picture—of which he (or she) forms but a small part of the background. One who is over-bearing, or of a scolding disposition, who does not apprehend the spirit of his work, who is slow in conclusion or tardy in execution, cannot hold the appreciation of the children or make the singing what it should be—delightful worship.

THE ORGANIST must be a skillful player, and possess the soul of expression,—whose mind and heart may go out to the singers above and beyond the mere manipulation of the key-board. The harmony should be played as written, as a Prelude, play the song itself, or a part thereof, with the melody well difined, and let the Interlude be a repetition of the last two or four measures of the song—not an attempt at elaboration.

THE SUPERINTENDENT, during the time allotted for singing, should alternate each song with a short Bible reading or concert recitation of Scripture, bearing upon the subject to follow. Open and close the school with a bright, cheerful song of praise—

"Clear the darkened windows, open wide the door,
Let the blessed sunshine in!"

SPECIAL MUSIC, such as Solos, Duets, Quartets, etc., should be judiciously introduced, for effect and variety; a solo with chorus by the school— a duet or quartet, to sing certain portions of a song alternately with the school—different classes and the school singing responsively. Various other forms might be mentioned that will greatly add to the musical interest, hold the attention and secure the cooperation of the entire school. In this collection will be found songs suited to almost every purpose and occasion.

Having been prepared especially **for** Sunday School work, "SUNSHINE" is now submitted.

CHAS. H. GABRIEL.

NOTICE:—Almost every song contained in this book is copyright property, and must not be reprinted or duplicated in any manner without the written permission of the owner of the copyright. MEYER & BROTHER.

SUNSHINE.

No. 1.   GOD IS LOVE.

CHAS. H. GABRIEL.   BEETHOVEN, arr.

1. Whisper'd by the ev'ning breeze, Chanted in the state-ly trees,
2. In the si-lence of the night, In the bu-sy morn-ing light,
3. 'Tis the theme of bird and bee, Flow'r, and breeze, and land, and sea;

Sung by brooklet in the vale, Shout-ed in the rag-ing gale,
In the murm'rings on the shore, In the crash-ing thunder's roar,
Ev-'ry thing in rap-ture cries, And the ans-wer from the skies,

Hear it ringing:—"God is love!" Gladness bringing, "God is love!"
Hear it pealing:—"God is love!" Soft-ly steal-ing, "God is love!"
Tells the sto-ry:—"God is love!" Speaks His glo-ry, "God is love!"

REFRAIN.

Sweet-est words be-low,—a-bove; "God is wis-dom, God is love."

WORDS AND ARRANGEMENT OF MUSIC COPYRIGHT, 1895, BY CHAS. H. GABRIEL.

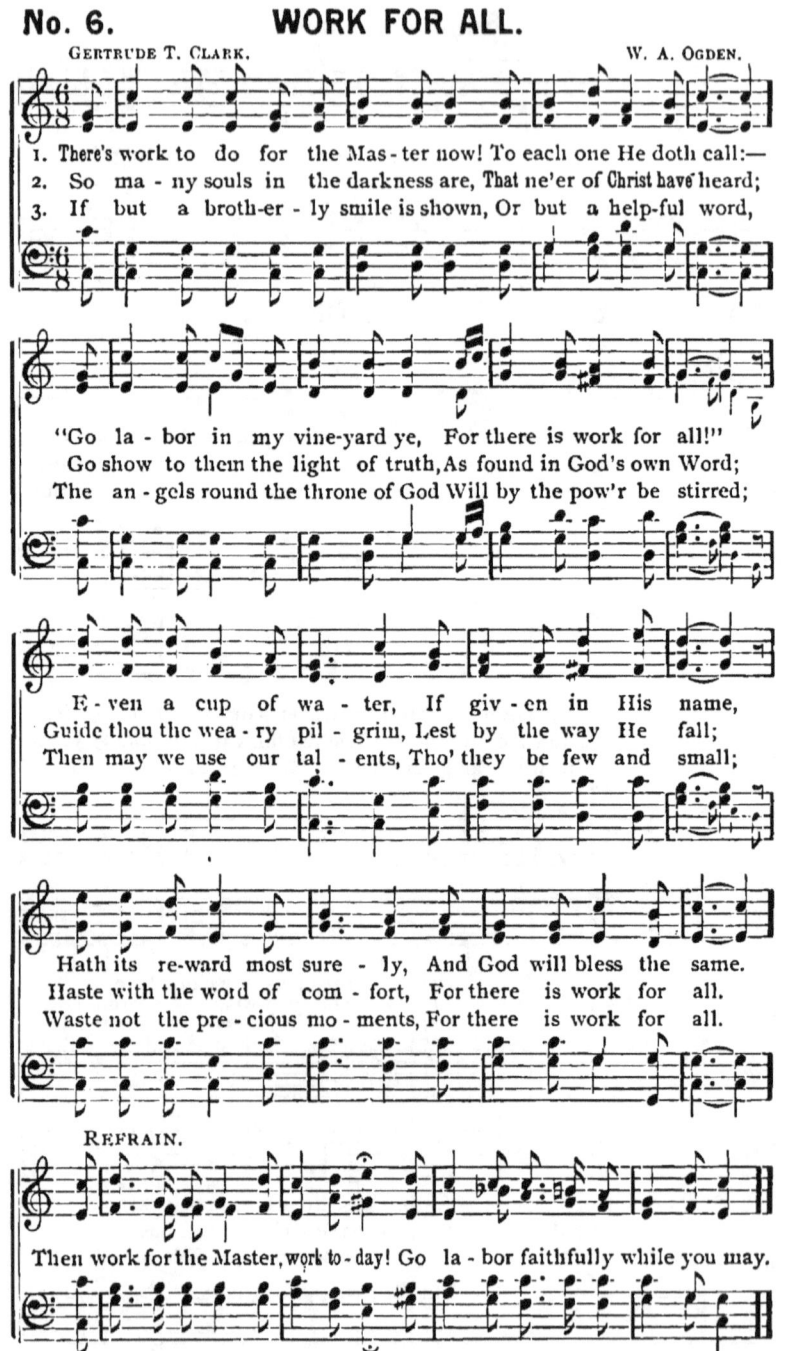

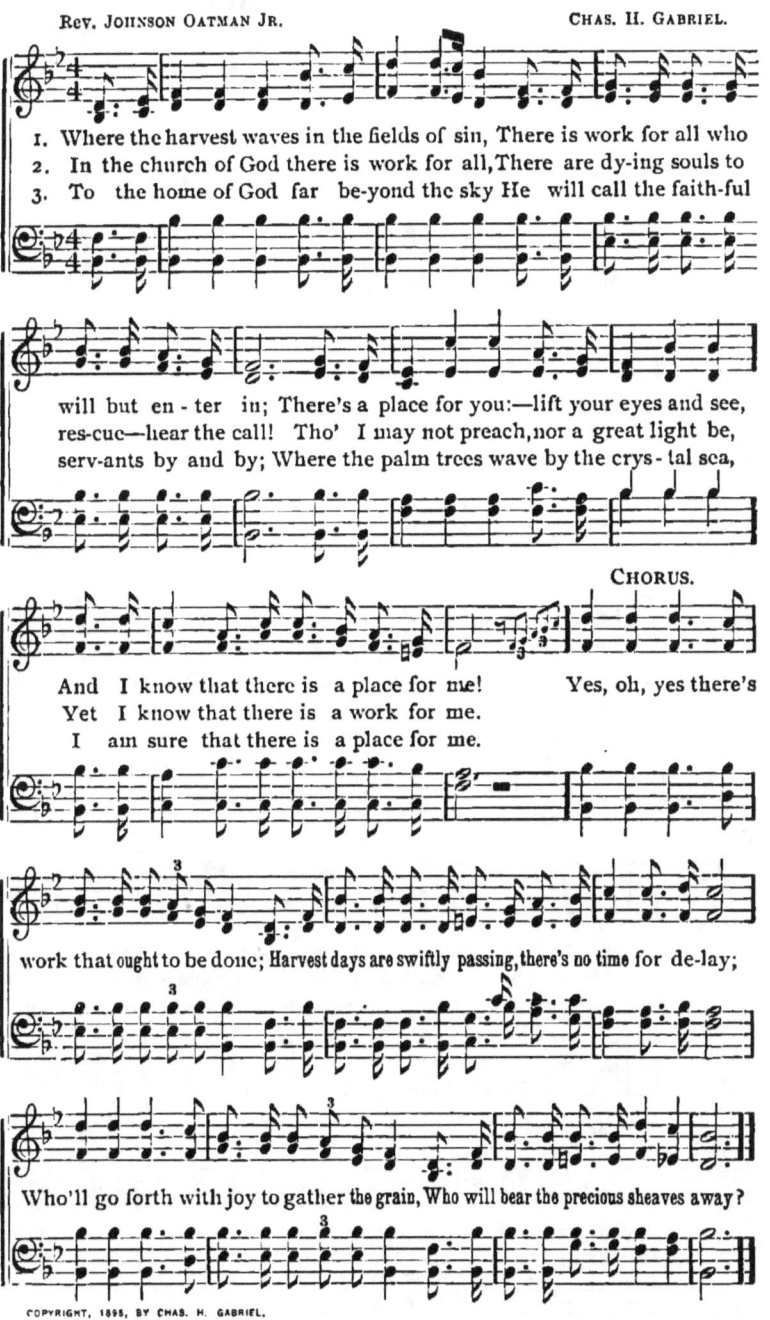

Praise the Lord.

From millions gone before us, Praise, oh, praise the Lord!
From the mill-ions gone be-fore us,

No. 9. DARE TO DO RIGHT.

CHAS. H. GABRIEL.

1. Dare to think, tho' others frown; Dare in words your tho'ts express;
2. Dare from cus-tom to de-part; Dare the priceless pearl pos-sess;
3. Dare forsake what you deem wrong; Dare to walk in wis-dom's way;

Dare to rise tho' oft cast down; Dare the wronged and scorned to bless.
Dare to wear it next your heart; Dare, when others curse, to bless.
Dare to give where gifts be-long; Dare God's pre-cepts to o-bey.

CHORUS.

Do what conscience says is right, Do what rea-son says is best,
Do what con-science says is right, Do what reason says is best,

Do with all your mind and heart, Do your du-ty and be blest.
Do with all your mind and heart, Do your du-ty and be blest.

COPYRIGHT, 1890, BY CHAS. H. GABRIEL.

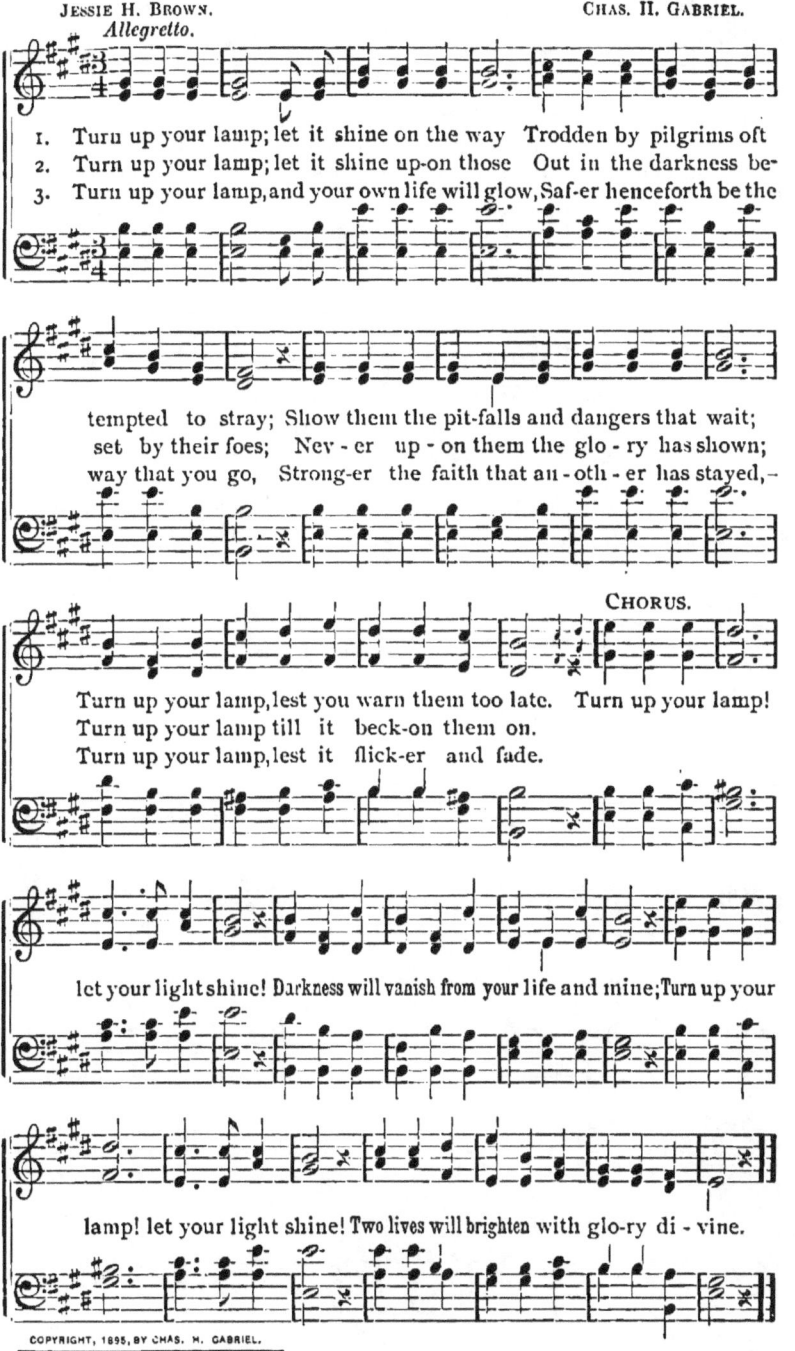

No. 12. SHOULDER TO SHOULDER.

E. E. Hewitt.   Wm. J. Kirkpatrick.

1. Shoul-der to shoulder, Pressing on with pray'r; One the road we journey,
2. Shoul-der to shoulder, In the work of life; Nev-er room for en-vy,
3. Shoul-der to shoulder, One in blest ac-cord, Fol-low-ing our Mas-ter,

One the name we bear. One great foe confronts us, 'Tis the host of sin;
Nev-er time for strife. Faith-ful, true and earnest, On the whit'ning field,
Wor-ship-ing one Lord. Closer grows our un-ion; Oh, the might-y bond!

CHORUS.

One great faith u-nites us; On-ly thus we win. Marching, marching,
So shall christian la-bor Gold-en harvests yield.
One sweet love constraining, One bright home a-bove.

marching on to-geth-er, Working, working, working hand in hand; Marching, marching,

on to ho-ly war-fare, On to brightest glo-ry in Immanuel's land.

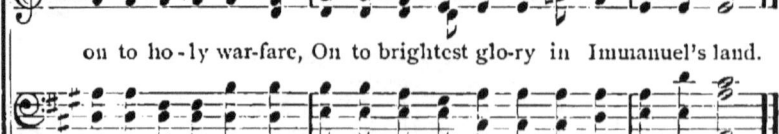

Copyright, 1889, by Wm. J. Kirkpatrick.

No. 21. CLINGING TO HIS PROMISE.

IDA L. REED. PHILIP PHILLIPS, MUS. DOC.

1. Cling-ing to His prom-ise, Trust-ing in His word; Ev-er-more I'm rest-ing, Rest-ing in the Lord. Fol-low-ing His guid-ing, E'er con-tent to be In His love a-bid-ing, Thro' His mer-cy free.

2. Cling-ing to His prom-ise, Trust-ing more and more, Hiding in His shad-ow Till life's storms are o'er. List'ning to His coun-sel, Wait-ing at His feet; E'er His will o-bey-ing; O the hours are sweet.

3. Cling-ing to His prom-ise, Look-ing up to Him, Trusting in His guid-ance When the way is dim. Clouds may round me gath-er, But they can-not harm; He will keep me safe-ly, Shel-tered by His arm.

CHORUS.

Cling-ing to His prom-ise, Trusting day by day, Glad-ly I'll go forward; Love will light the way.

COPYRIGHT, 1899, BY GEO. F. ROSCHE.

No. 22. THE SWEET OLDEN STORY.

M. S. K.
Rev. M. S. Kerby.

1. I have read of the sweet old-en sto-ry, Of the fair, hap-py E-den a-bove; Of the beau-ti-ful man-sions of glo-ry, In the bright golden cit-y of love.
2. I have read of the clear spark-ling riv-er, Burst-ing out 'neath the great throne of God; How its sweet waters glide on for-ev-er, Mak-ing glad all the host of the Lord.
3. I have read how the banks of that riv-er, By the saints and the an-gels are trod; How their glo-ri-ous an-thems for-ev-er, Swell the praise of our Savior and God.

CHORUS.

Oh, the sweet old-en sto-ry Of the fair, happy E-den a-bove; Of the beau-ti-ful mansions of glo-ry, In the bright golden cit-y of love.

COPYRIGHT, 1891, BY CHAS. H. GABRIEL.

No. 26. JESUS IS CALLING.

C. H. G.   CHAS. H. GABRIEL.

1. Je-sus is call-ing, lov-ing-ly call-ing, Mo-ments are wast-ing and the harvest is wide; Ma-ny are wait-ing, ma-ny are i-dle, Ma-ny are halt-ing, and a-wait-ing the tide.
2. Je-sus is call-ing, lov-ing-ly call-ing, Gath-er the jew-els that in plen-ty are found; Tell the glad sto-ry, tell it with glad-ness, Un-til the world shall with His glo-ry re-sound.
3. Je-sus is call-ing, pa-tient-ly call-ing, En-ter the field, joy-ful-ly sing-ing his love; Comfort the weak ones, res-cue the wand-'rer, Tell the glad sto-ry of the mansions a-bove.

CHORUS.

Jesus is call-ing, so lovingly call-ing, Enter the field, for there's plen-ty to do, ... Take up the cross, and, no longer de-

Je-sus is call-ing, hear Him to-day, Enter the field for there's plen-ty to do, Take up the cross no

COPYRIGHT, 1892, BY GUIDE PRINTING & PUB CO.

Jesus is Calling.

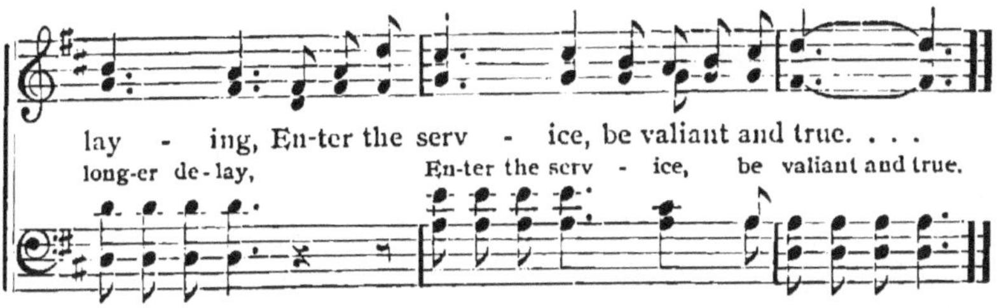

lay - ing, En-ter the serv - ice, be valiant and true. . . .
long-er de - lay, En-ter the serv - ice, be valiant and true.

No. 27. WHAT A BLESSED SALVATION.

E. E. HEWITT. EMMA E. MEYER.

1. In Christ is full redemption found, What a bless-ed sal - va-tion!
2. E - ter - nal life thro' Je-sus' blood, What a bless-ed sal - va-tion!
3. He takes my crimson stains a - way, What a bless-ed sal - va-tion!
4. Sweet peace amid the world's rude strife, What a bless-ed sal - va-tion!
5. His ev - er - last-ing grace proclaim, What a bless-ed sal - va-tion!

His prais-es thro' my soul re-sound, What a bless - ed sal - va-tion!
Come, sink be-neath the crimson flood, What a bless - ed sal - va-tion!
He helps and keeps me ev - 'ry day, What a bless - ed sal - va-tion!
Tri-umph-ant joy be - yond this life, What a bless - ed sal - va-tion!
Thro' endless days we'll sing His name, What a bless - ed sal - va-tion!

CHORUS.

What a blessed salvation in Christ, my Redeemer! for sin-ners like me.

COPYRIGHT, 1895, BY MEYER & BROTHER.

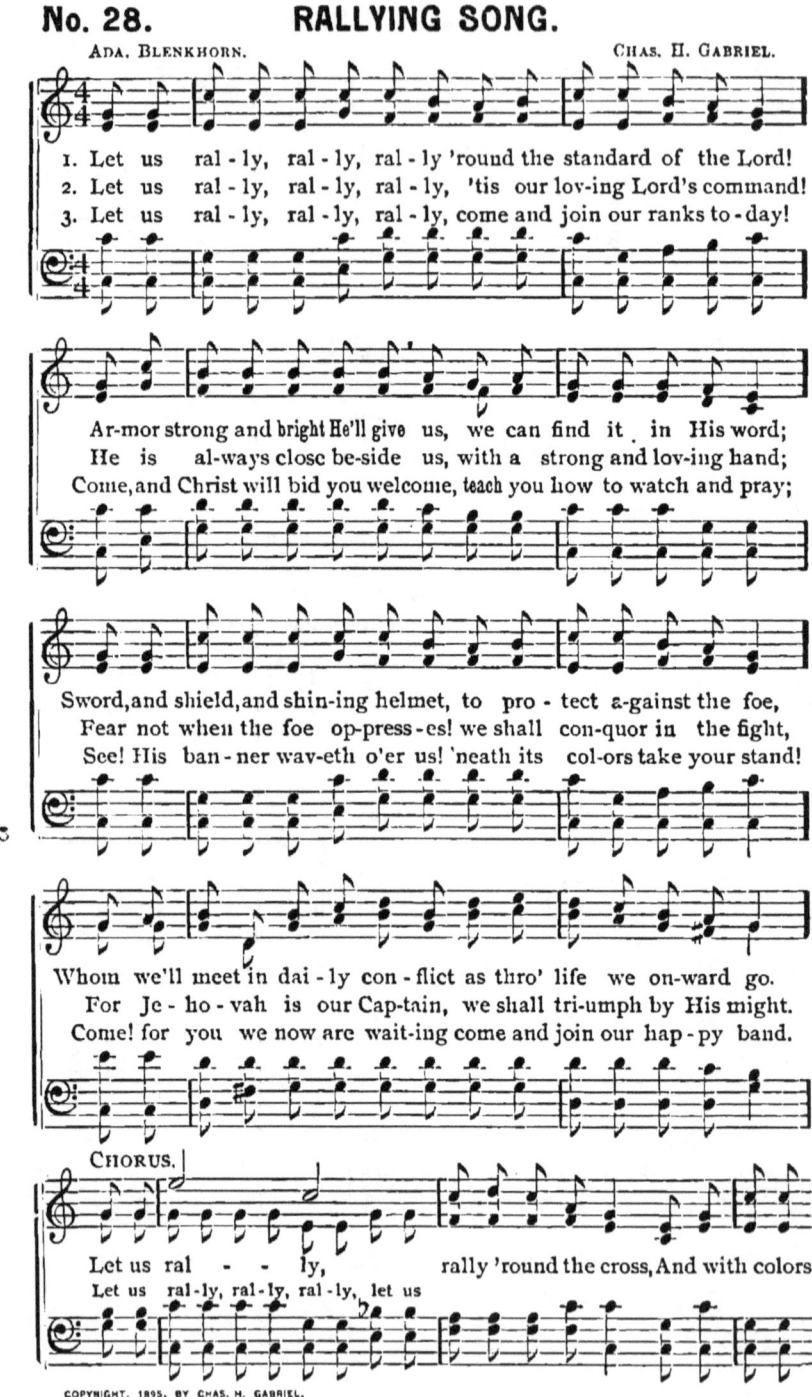

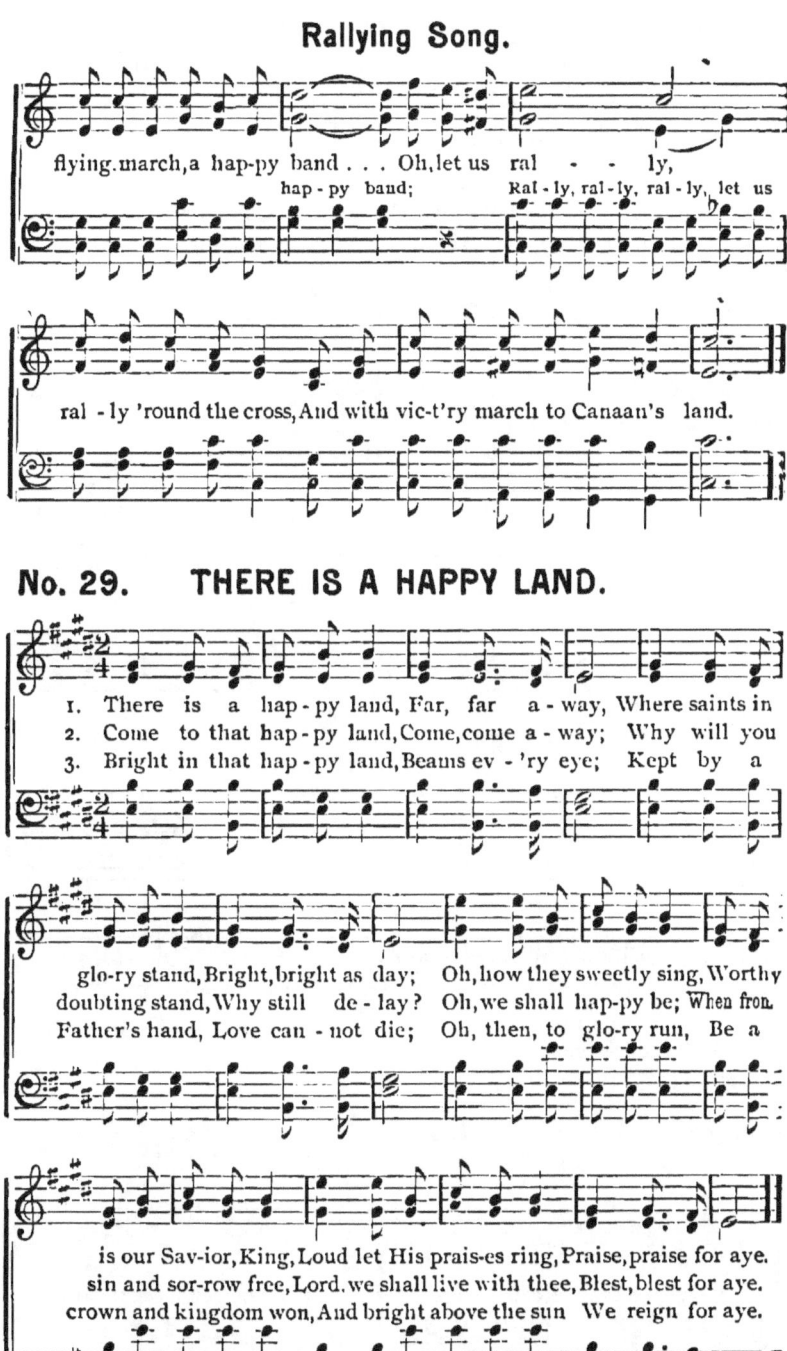

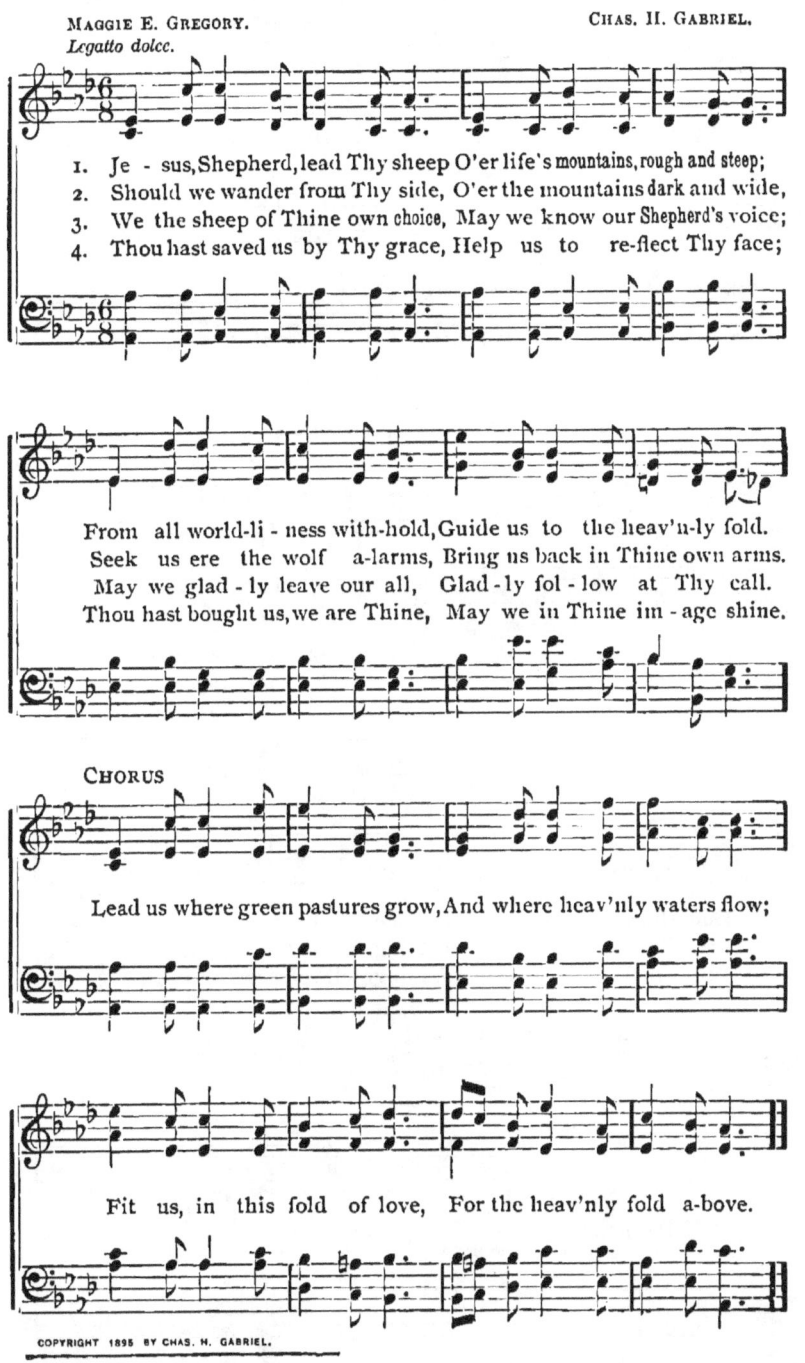

Be Not Afraid.

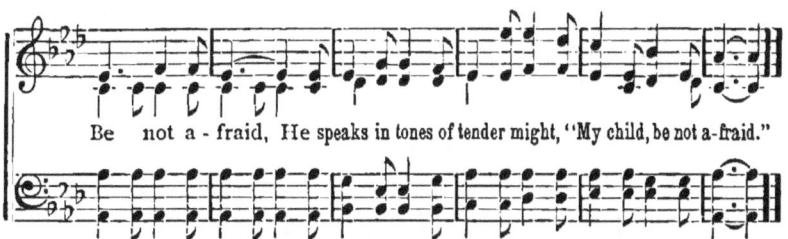

Be not a-fraid, He speaks in tones of tender might, "My child, be not a-fraid."

No. 41. SINGING, SPEAKING, PRAYING.

ADA BLENKHORN.   Dr. S. B. JACKSON.

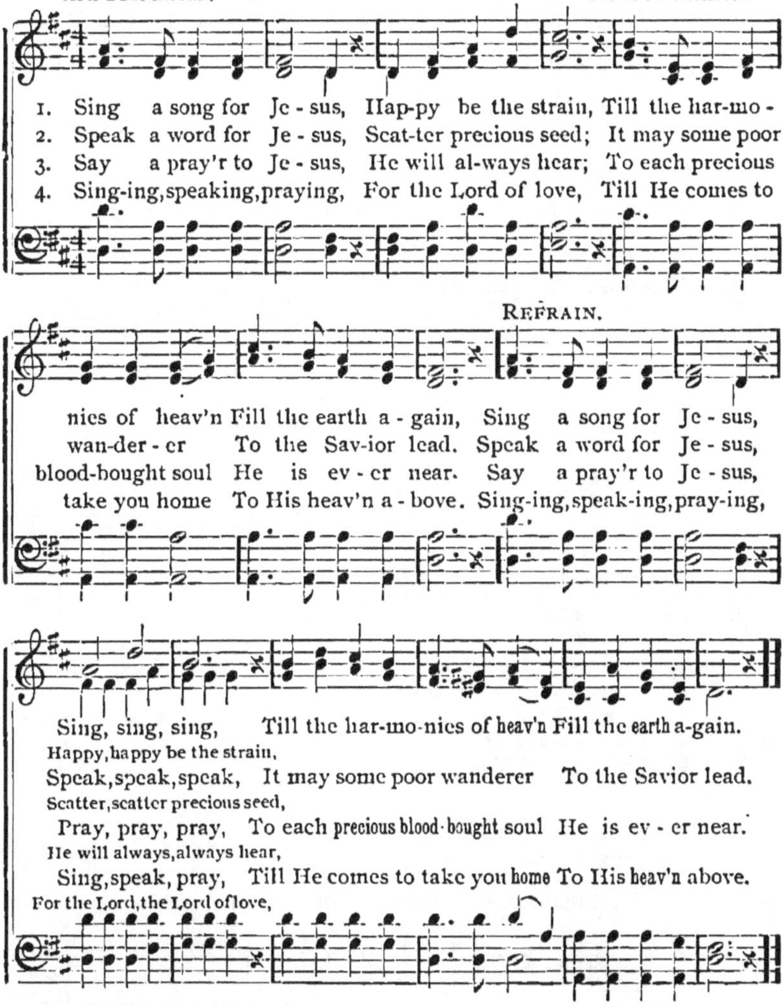

1. Sing a song for Je-sus, Hap-py be the strain, Till the har-mo-
2. Speak a word for Je-sus, Scat-ter precious seed; It may some poor
3. Say a pray'r to Je-sus, He will al-ways hear; To each precious
4. Sing-ing, speaking, praying, For the Lord of love, Till He comes to

REFRAIN.

nies of heav'n Fill the earth a-gain, Sing a song for Je-sus,
wan-der-er To the Sav-ior lead. Speak a word for Je-sus,
blood-bought soul He is ev-er near. Say a pray'r to Je-sus,
take you home To His heav'n a-bove. Sing-ing, speak-ing, pray-ing,

Sing, sing, sing, Till the har-mo-nies of heav'n Fill the earth a-gain.
Happy, happy be the strain,
Speak, speak, speak, It may some poor wanderer To the Savior lead.
Scatter, scatter precious seed,
Pray, pray, pray, To each precious blood-bought soul He is ev-er near.
He will always, always hear,
Sing, speak, pray, Till He comes to take you home To His heav'n above.
For the Lord, the Lord of love,

COPYRIGHT, 1895, BY CHAS. H. GABRIEL.

No. 43. SCATTER SEED.

x. x. x.
J. L. Moore.

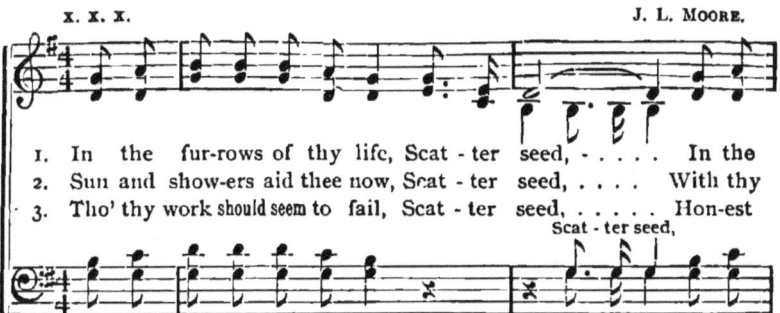

1. In the fur-rows of thy life, Scat-ter seed, ... In the
2. Sun and show-ers aid thee now, Scat-ter seed, ... With thy
3. Tho' thy work should seem to fail, Scat-ter seed, ... Hon-est

Scat-ter seed,

midst of toil and strife, Scatter seed!   Small may be thy spir-it field,
hand up-on the plow, Scatter seed!   Who can tell where grain may grow!
purpose will a-vail, Scatter seed!   Some may fall on stony ground:

Scat-ter seed!

D. S.—furrows of thy life, Scatter seed!   Small may be thy spirit field,

FINE.

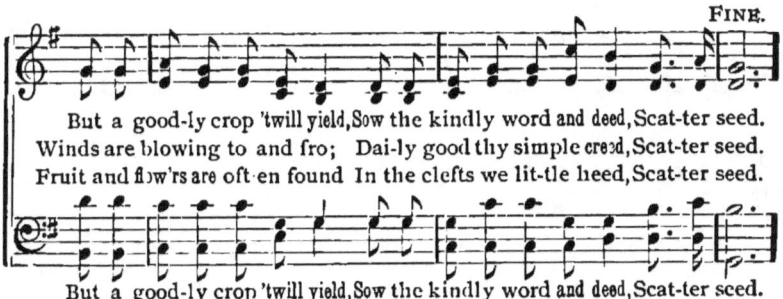

But a good-ly crop 'twill yield, Sow the kindly word and deed, Scat-ter seed.
Winds are blowing to and fro; Dai-ly good thy simple creed, Scat-ter seed.
Fruit and flow'rs are oft-en found In the clefts we lit-tle heed, Scat-ter seed.

But a good-ly crop 'twill yield, Sow the kindly word and deed, Scat-ter seed.

CHORUS.   D. S.

Scat-ter seed, ... scat-ter seed; ..... In the
Scat-ter seed of good, yes, scat-ter, scat-ter seed;

COPYRIGHT, 1890, BY CHAS. H. GABRIEL.

He Loves Them.

words un-to us He hath giv-en—"O such is the kingdom of heaven."

No. 45. HOLD ME IN THY CARE.

WILLARD P. MORRIS.

1. Lamb of God I look to Thee, Thou shalt my ex-am-ple be;
2. Fain I would be as Thou art, Give to me th' o-be-dient heart;
3. I shall then show forth Thy praise, Serve Thee all my hap-py days,

Thou art ho-ly, meek and mild, I am but a sin-ful child.
Thou art pit-i-ful and kind, Let me have Thy lov-ing mind.
And the world shall know and see That Thy spir-it dwells in me.

REFRAIN.

Hold ..... me Sav - ior, In Thy lov-ing care,
Hold me, hold me Sav-ior dear,

Keep me from temp-ta-tion, More than I can bear.

COPYRIGHT, 1891, BY R. M. MCINTOSH

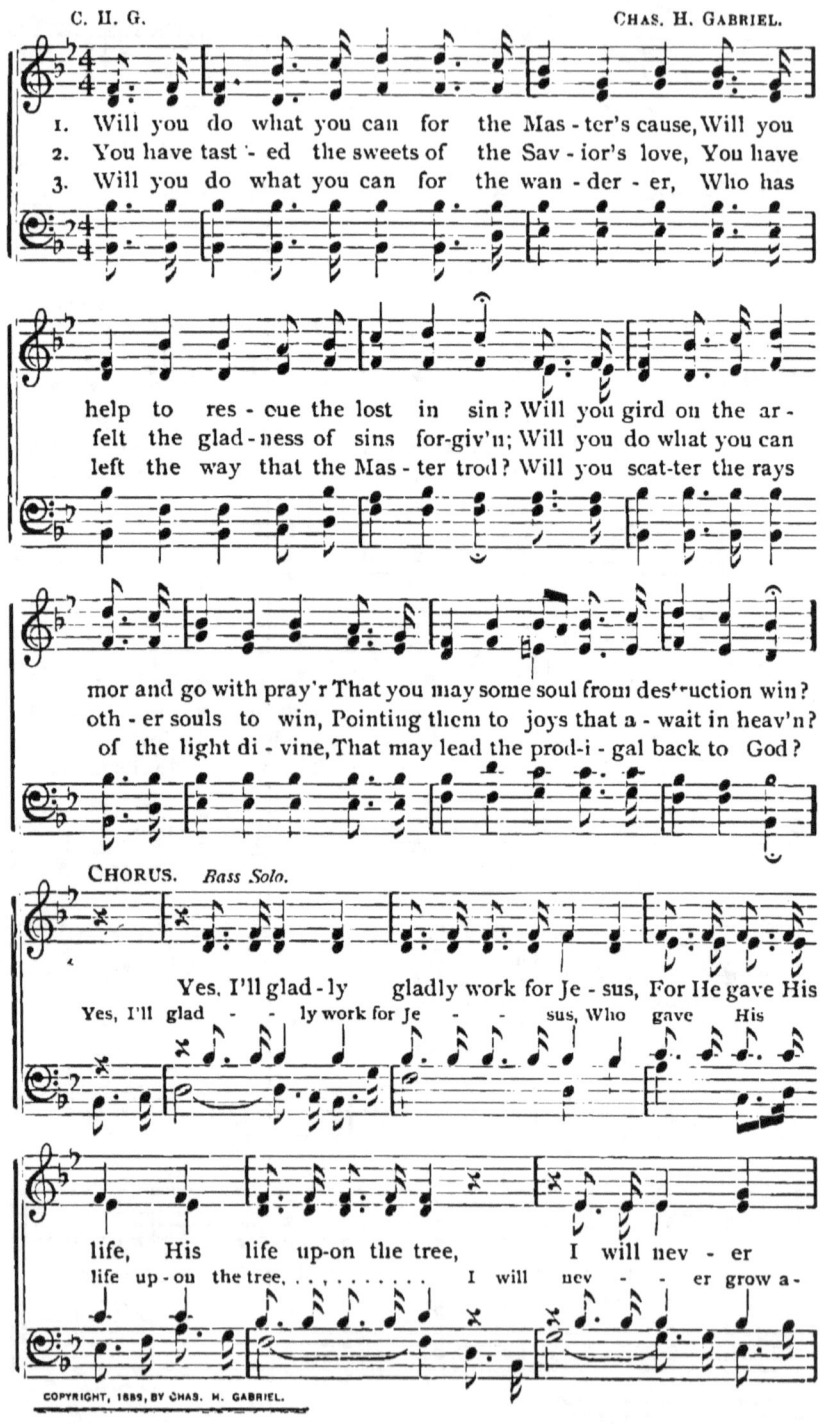

No. 49. **GATHER IN THE GRAIN.**

Charlotte G. Homer.　　　　　　　　　　　　James McGranahan.

1. Go, gath-er in the gold-en grain, for, lo, 'tis har-vest time: The call comes ring-ing o'er the world from ev-'ry land and clime. The fields are white to har-vest, but the reap-ers,—where are they? Up, for the Lord of har-vest calls to work, to work to-day!
2. Go, gath-er in the gold-en grain,—a faith-ful reap-er be; Take down the rust-y sick-le, for the Lord hath need of thee. Go out in-to the high-ways and the hedg-es ev-'ry-where, And gath-er in the pre-cious sheaves that lie neg-lect-ed there.
3. Go, gath-er in the gold-en grain,—your du-ty is as-signed; Be faith-ful in the cause of right,—the good of hu-man kind. Go, speak a word of com-fort sweet to some one in dis-tress, And He who raised the wid-ow's son, a-bund-ant-ly will bless.

CHORUS.

Go, gath-er in the grain from valley, hill and plain; Make no delay, the call obey—Go, gather in the grain.

MUSIC COPYRIGHT, 1875, BY Z. M. PARVIN. WORDS AND RE-ISSUE OF MUSIC COPYRIGHT, 1894, BY CHAS. H. GABRIEL, OWNER.

Loyal and True.

1. Let me a sow-er be, Let me a mow-er be— And to our
2. Let me a preacher be, Let me a teacher be— And to our
3. Then let me ev-er sing, Joy to some heart to bring, And to our

great Com-mand-er loy-al be and true, Oh, let me a sow-er be,
great Com-mand-er loy-al be and true, Oh, let me a preacher be,
great Com-mand-er loy-al be and true, Oh, then let me ev-er sing,

Let me a mow-er be, Read-y to do what-ev-er I may find to do.
Let me a teach-er be, Read-y to do what-ev-er I may find to do.
Joy to some heart to bring, Read-y to do what-ev-er I may find to do.

No. 51. THE LORD'S PRAYER.

1. Our Father which art in heaven, hallowed | be Thy name, ‖Thy kingdom come, Thy will be done in | earth, as it | is in | heaven.
2. Give us this day our | daily | bread, ‖And forgive us our trespasses, as we forgive | them that | trespass a- | gainst us.
3. And lead us not into temptation, but deliver | us from ! evil;‖For Thine is the kingdom, and the power and the | glory for- | ever and | ever ‖A- | men.

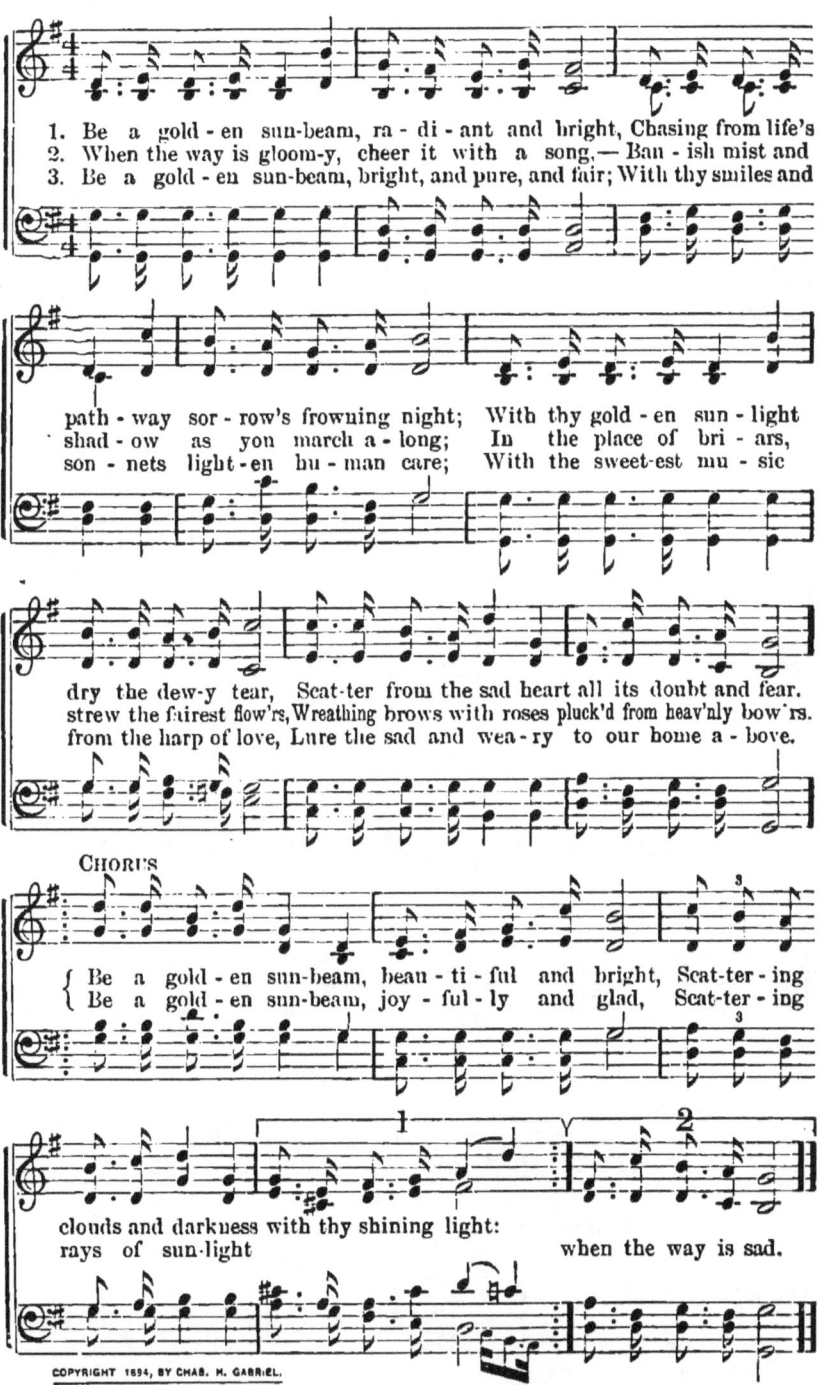

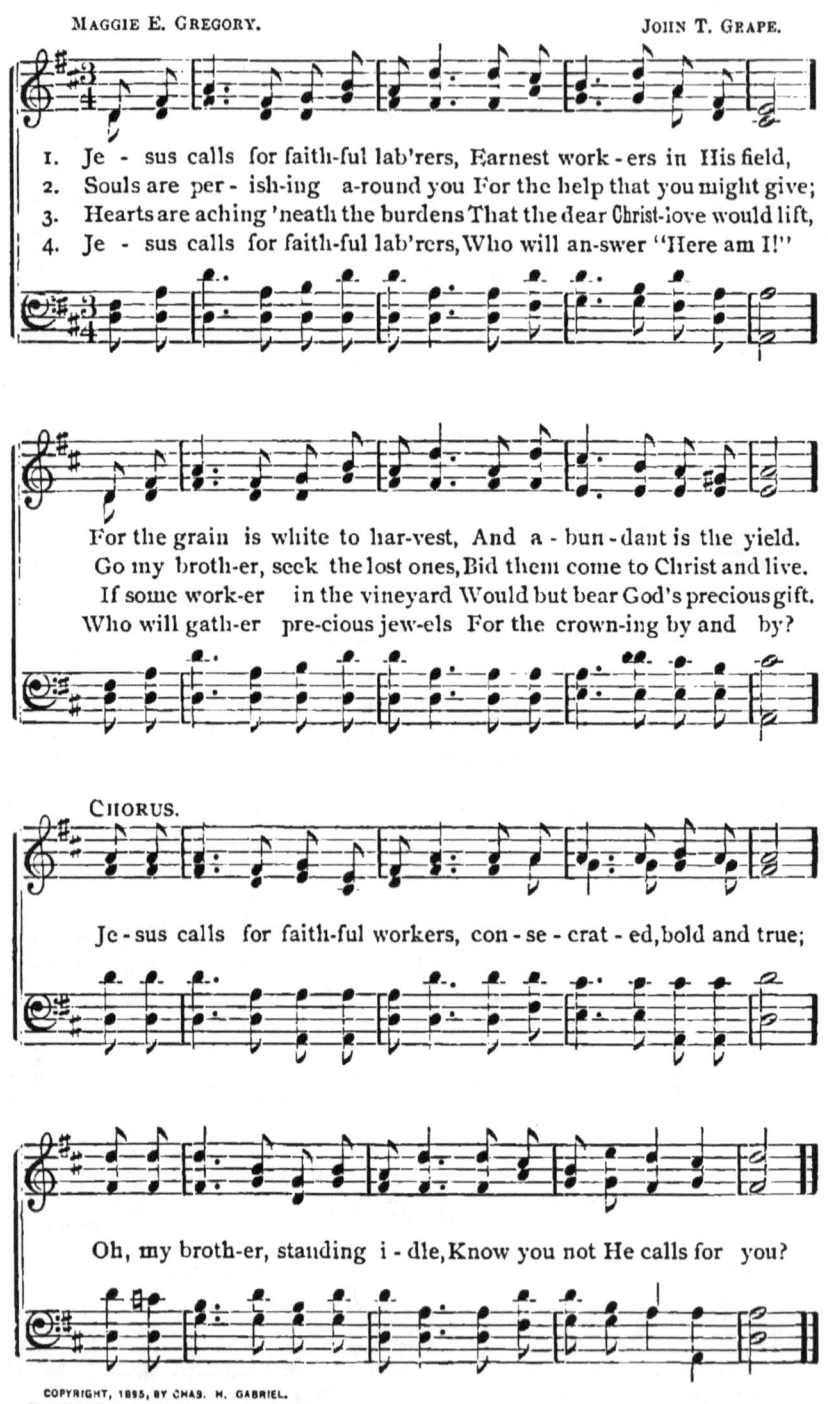

No. 58. THE LIGHT OF THE CROSS.

CHARLOTTE G. HOMER.
March tempo.
CHAS. H. GABRIEL.

1. From the cross of Christ up-lift-ed Shines an ev-er-last-ing light;
2. Ev-'ry storm that gath-ers o'er us, Adds new lus-ter to its ray;
3. Tho' the tem-pest 'round me rages, By its light my way is sure;

By its rays the clouds are rift-ed, 'Til the home-land is in sight.
And the cares that rise be-fore us, In its radiance pass a-way.
And thro'-out the sweep of a-ges, It, un-shak-en, shall en-dure.

CHORUS.

Bless-ed light, light di-vine, To the world thy rays are
Bless-ed light, light di-vine,

stream-ing; Hallowed light, light of love, From the
Hal-lowed light, light of love,

QUARTET. (*May be omitted.*)

cross of Christ is beam-ing, Oh, thou bright and shining light, gleam
Beautiful light,

COPYRIGHT, 1895, BY CHAS. H. GABRIEL.

Glorious News.

Car-ry the mes-sage to lands far a-way! Tell the glad news, the glo-rious news, We have a Sav-ior who's liv-ing to-day.
glo - rious news,

No. 61. BATTLE HYMN OF MISSIONS.

RAY PALMER.   JOHN WHITAKER.

1. E-ter-nal Fa-ther, Thou hast said, That Christ all glo-ry shall ob-tain; That He who once a suf-f'rer bled, Shall o'er the world a con-qu'ror reign.
2. We wait Thy tri-umph, Sav-ior, King; Long a-ges have pre-pared Thy way; Now all a-broad thy ban-ner fling, Set time's great bat-tle in ar-ray.
3. Thy hosts are mus-tered to the field; "The Cross! the Cross!" the bat-tle call; The old grim tow'rs of dark-ness yield, And soon shall tot-ter to their fall.

No. 62. THE CHILD IN THE MIDST.

ADALINE HOHF BEERY. T. MARTIN TOWNE.

1. When Je-sus was asked by His ser-vants of old, To whom shall the
2. Tho' hon-or and rich-es may brighten our way, Our friends true and
3. God bless-es the chil-dren because they are pure,—And all may be

great-ness be giv'n? He beckoned a lit-tle one to Him and said,
loy-al re-main, Ex-cept we are will-ing the poor-est to serve,
such, by His grace; Thro' crosses and cares we may rise to His throne,

CHORUS.

"Of such is the king-dom of heav'n." Oh, Master, redeem us from
We can-not His king-dom at-tain.
And shine in the light of His face.

er-ror and pride, And make us a child in thy sight; With meekness and

trust may our bo-som be filled, And love guide our actions a-right.

COPYRIGHT, 1891, BY GEO. F. ROSCHE.

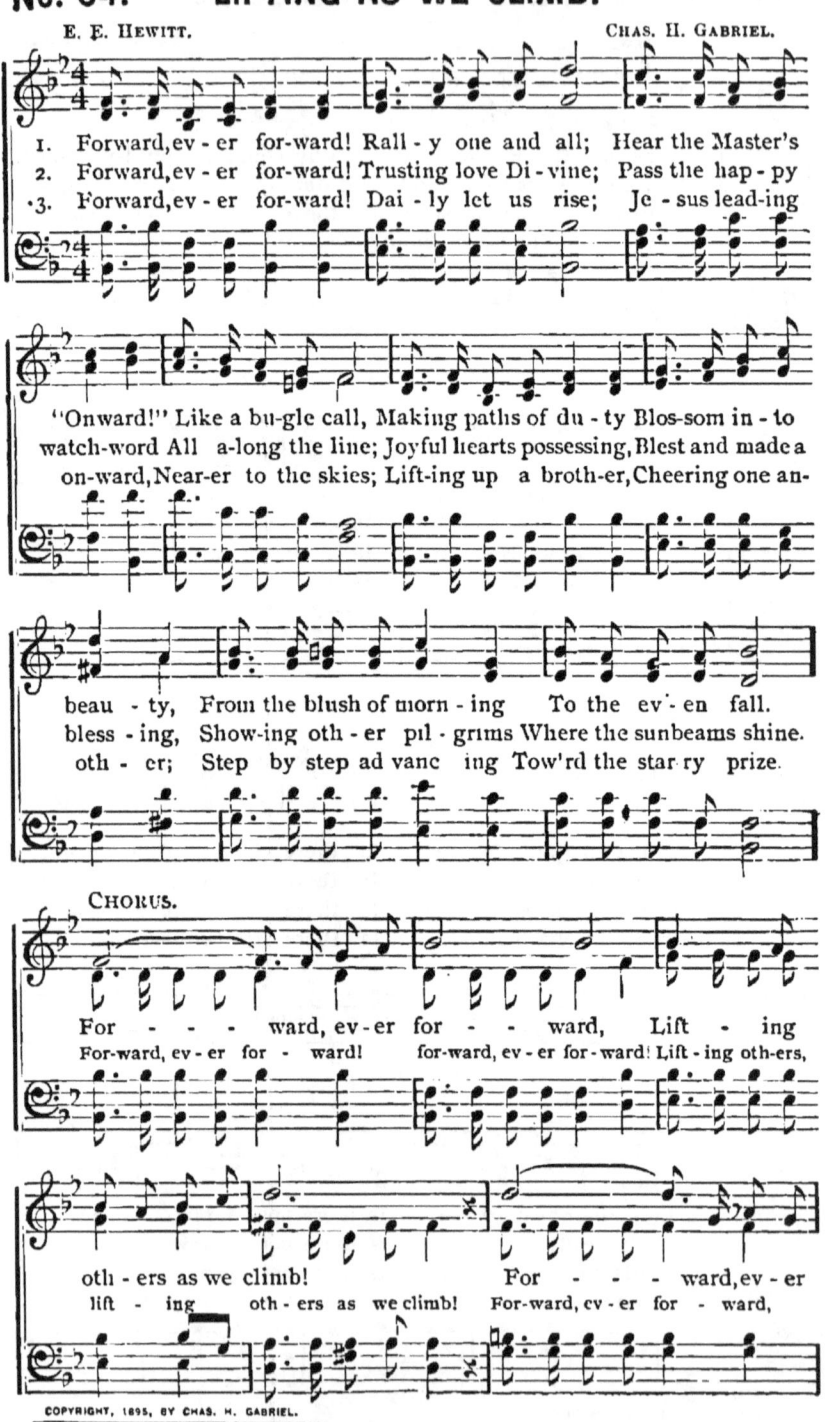

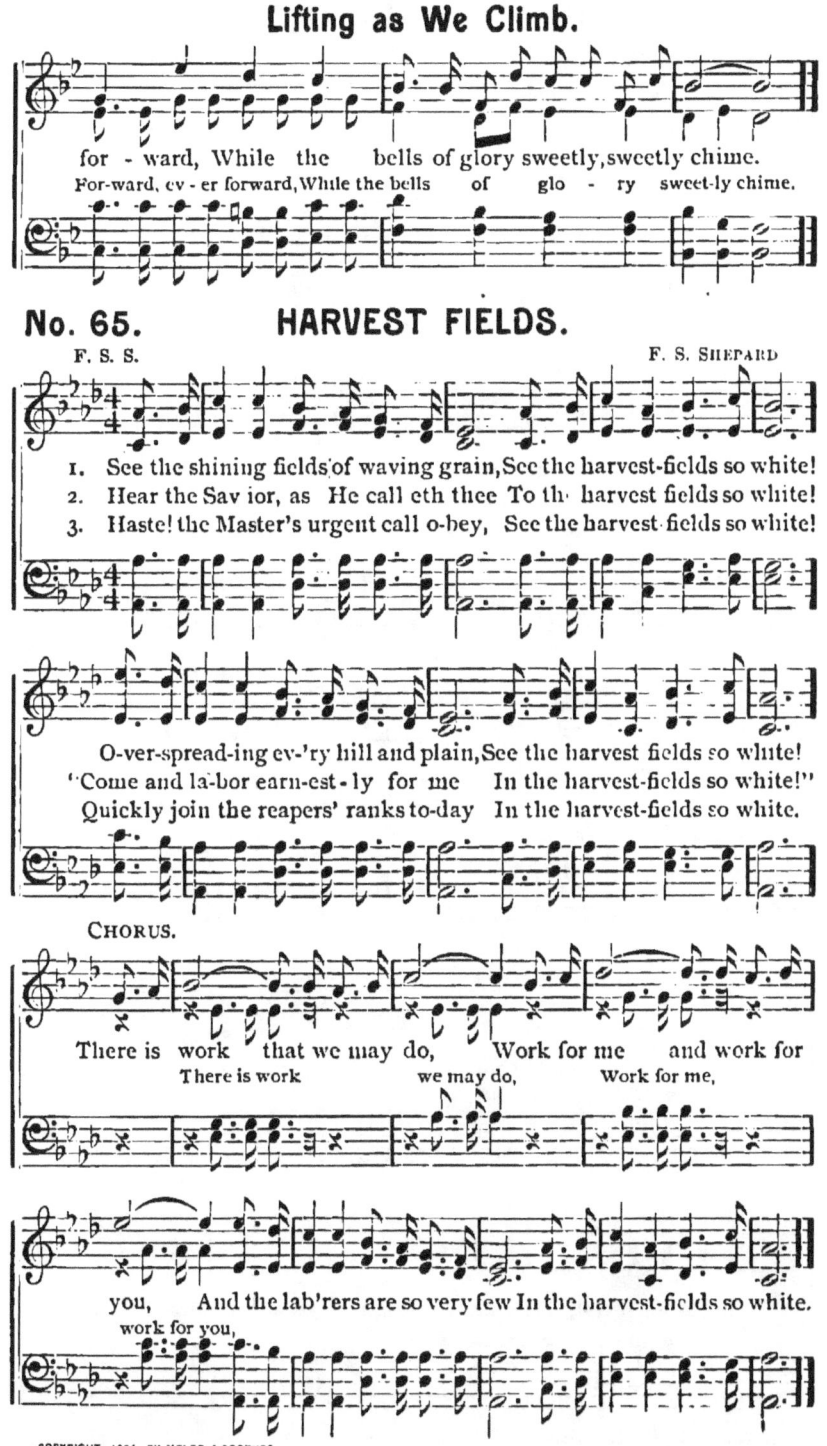

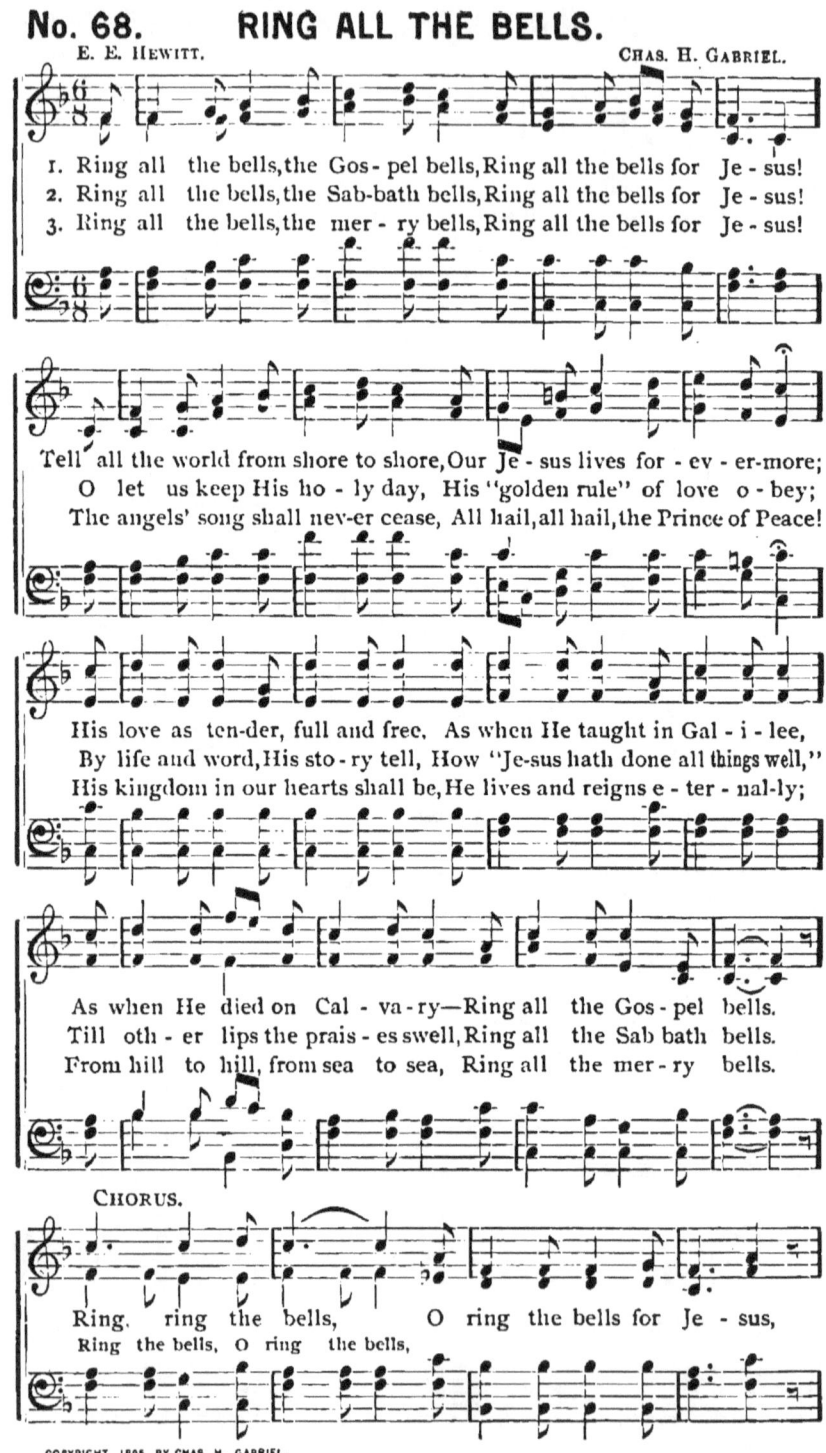

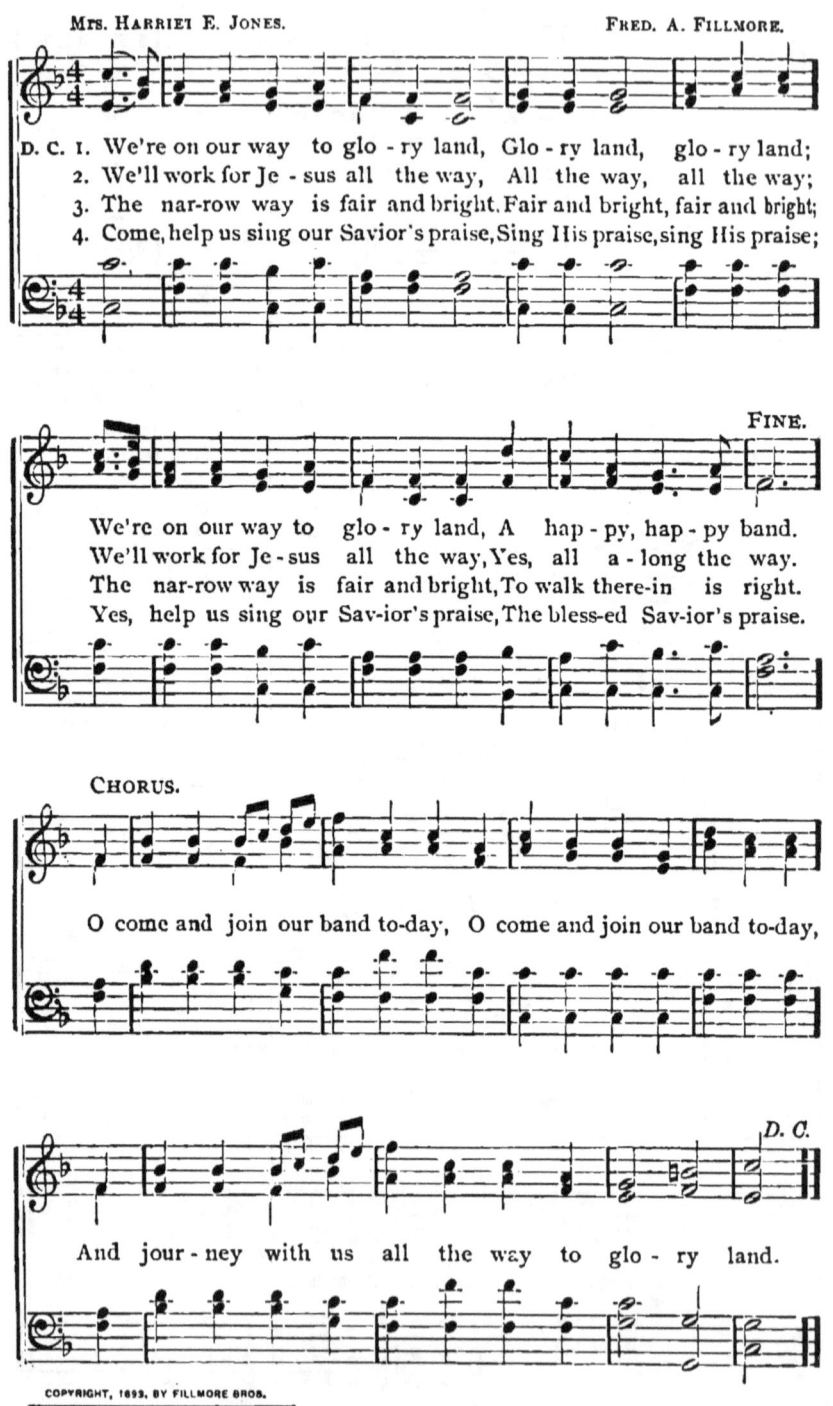

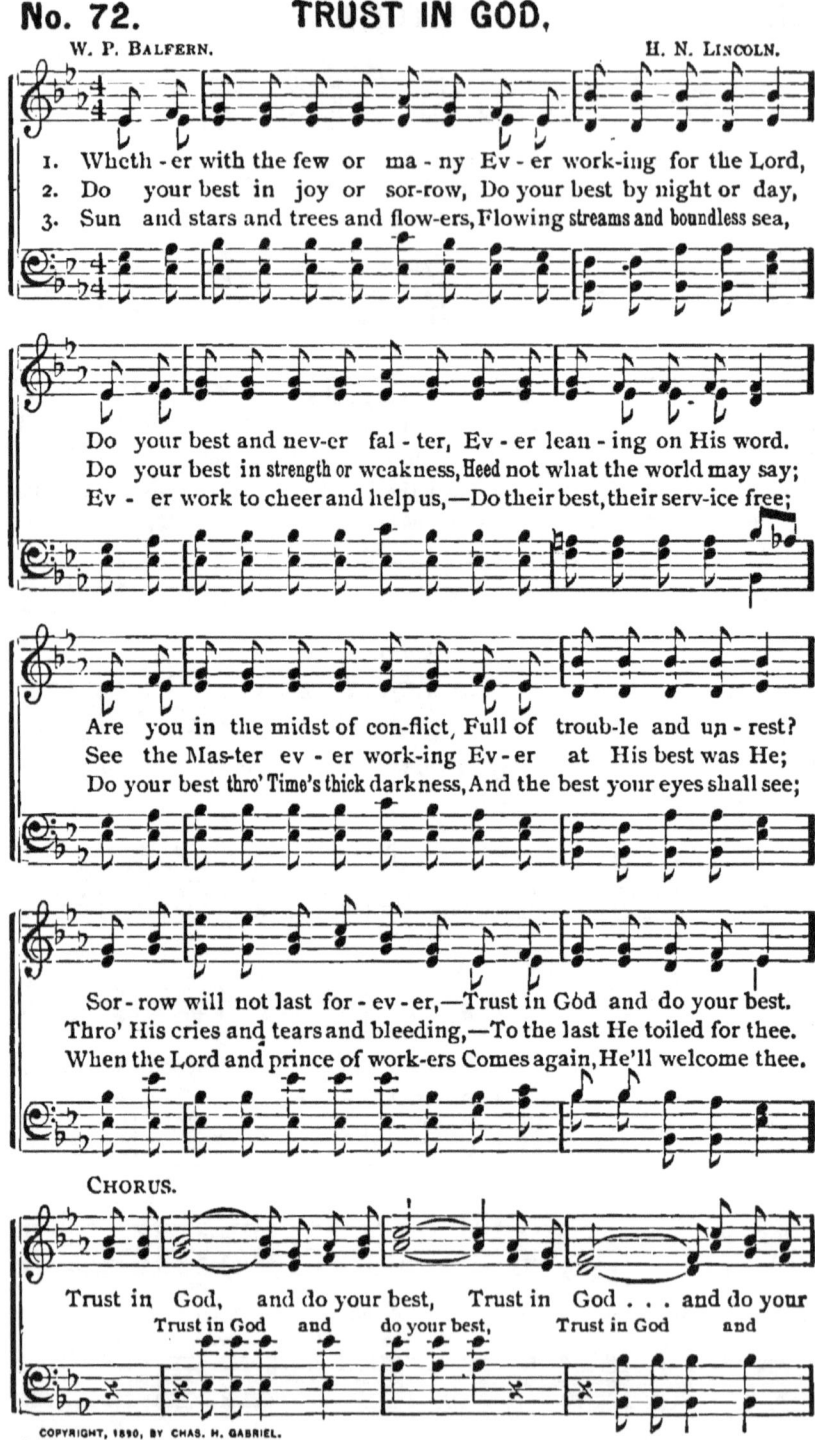

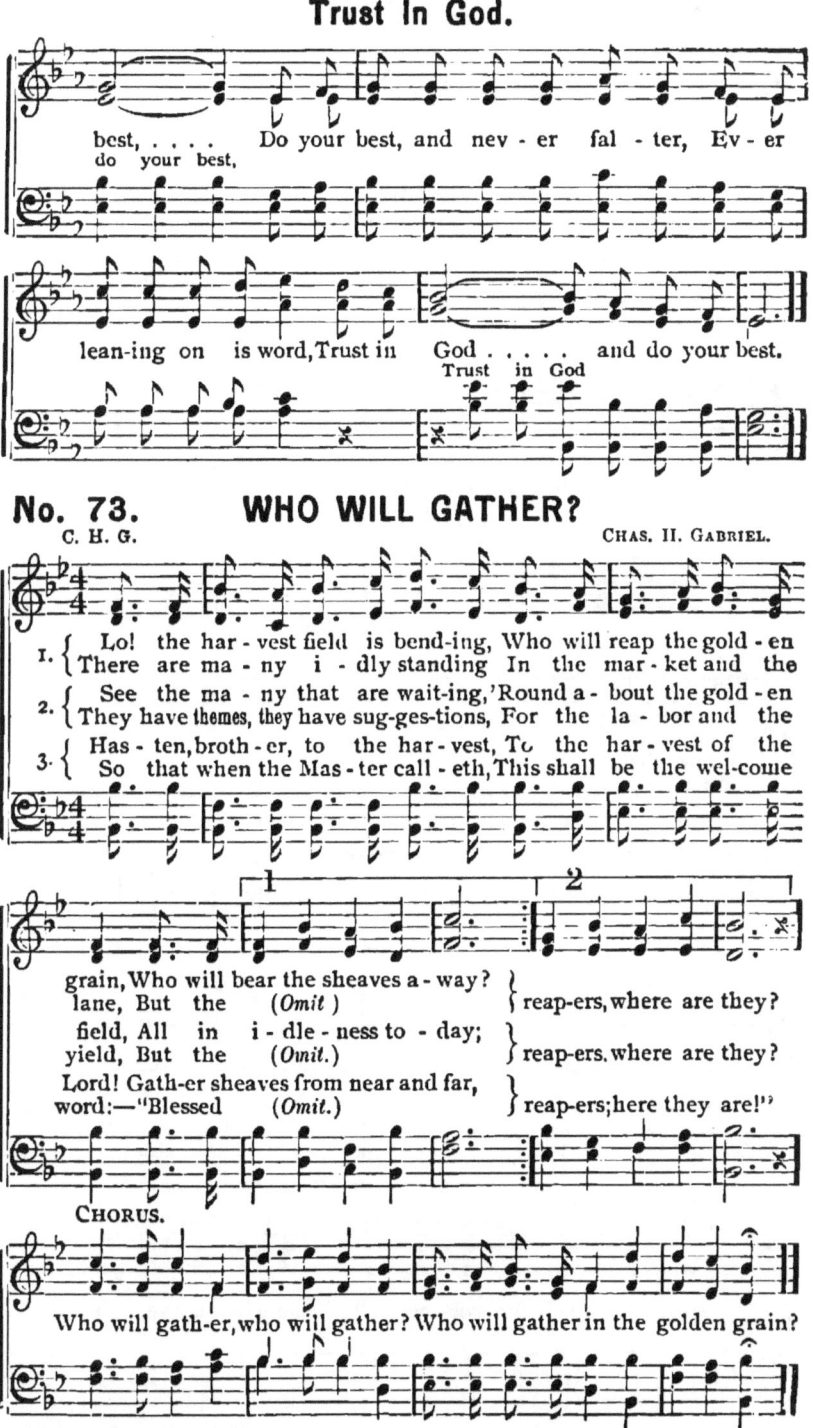

No. 74. **ROOM FOR THEE.**

E. E. Hewitt.   Chas. H. Gabriel.

1. Room e-nough at Calv'ry 'neath the crim-son flow! At the cross of Je-sus humbly bend-ing low, Oth-ers find sal-va-tion, from their bur-dens free, Still the lov-ing Spir-it calls for thee.
2. Room e-nough for serv-ice in the vineyard wide, Work to do for Je-sus—needful pow'r supplied; In the near-est du-ty, in the dai-ly care, Find a mis-sion, find a bless-ing there.
3. Room e-nough in glo-ry, when the work is done, At the marriage sup-per of the roy-al Son; In the shin-ing man-sions by the crys-tal sea, Room for all, and room e-nough for thee.

CHORUS.

Room enough, room enough, room e-nough for all; Room for ev-'ry soul who heeds the gos-pel call; Come while mer-cy lin-gers,

Copyright, 1895, by Chas. H. Gabriel.

Room for Thee.

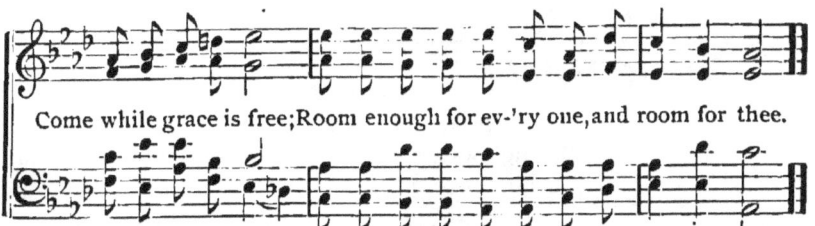

Come while grace is free; Room enough for ev-'ry one, and room for thee.

No. 75. CHILDREN'S BATTLE SONG.

Mrs. FRANK G. GOODWIN.   C. D. E.

1. O Je-sus, might-y Cap-tain, Thy sol-diers we would be,
2. Thy shield of faith and pow-er, Thine ar-mor from a-bove;
3. Then keep us ev-er faith-ful, A-lert, and brave, and strong

For Thy great vic-t'ries may be won By chil-dren such as we.
These would we wear, while floateth to The world our ban-ner, "Love."
To hear our Cap-tain's or-ders, and To con-quor sin and wrong.

CHORUS.

We'll fight, for the foe is watch-ful, We'll fight, for the foe is strong;

With Je-sus to lead us on-ward, The struggle will not be long.

COPYRIGHT, 1895, BY CHAS. H. GABRIEL.

No. 78. STEER TOWARD THE LIGHT.

GERTRUDE T. CLARK.   W. A. OGDEN.

1. Fierce is the tem-pest, loud is its roar, Storm-tossed the mar-in-er,
2. Storms cannot hide it, years can-not fade; Firm its foun-da-tion is,
3. When wild the tem-pest round thee is hurled, Look un-to Je-sus, the

far from the shore; See! what is put-ting the dark-ness to flight?
be not a-fraid; Heav'n's ample har-bor shall soon greet thy sight,
hope of the world; Bright shall the day be that fol-lows the night,

CHORUS.

Je-sus, the Morning Star; steer t'ward the light!
Watch for the dawn of day, steer t'ward the light! } Brightly it gleams, and its
Cour-age, then, mar-in-er, steer t'ward the light!

pure sil-ver beams Scat-ter the gloom of the night, of the night; Tho' the

storms round thee rave, He is mighty to save, Then, mariner, steer t'ward the light.

COPYRIGHT, 1899, BY CHAS. H. GABRIEL.

No. 79. SONG OF THE SAVIOR.

Dr. S. Fillmore Bennett.   Chas. H. Gabriel.

1. Sing we a song of the Sav-ior, Gentle, and lov-ing, and true,
2. Born in the Beth-le-hem man-ger, An-gels at-tend-ed His birth,
3. Bear-ing His bur-den of sor-rows, Still did He love us the same;
4. Now to the heav-ens as-cend-ed, Him by the Fa-ther be-hold,

Walk-ing the val-ley of shad-ows, Dy-ing for me and for you.
And from the heav-ens de-scend-ed Songs of re-joic-ing to earth.
All that re-viled Him for-giv-ing, Bear-ing the cross and its shame.
Plead-ing the cause of His chil-dren, Lov-ing us just as of old.

Chorus.

Praise Him, praise Him, Gen-tle, and lov-ing, and true;

Praise Him, praise Him, Dy-ing for me and for you.

Copyright, 1893, by Chas. H. Gabriel.

No. 82. JESUS LEADS THE WAY.

ADA BLENHORN.   CHAS. H. GABRIEL.

1. Go forth to the work, 'tis the Sav-ior's command; And, trust-ing His ev-er-last-ing name, Go out o-ver mountain and val-ley and plain, His grace and His mighty love proclaim; Where souls in the dreary night of darkness are dwelling. In dis-tant islands of the sea, Go ye with lov-ing heart, and joy-ful-ly tell them, Je-sus alone can make them free.

2. Go forth to the work, ev - er val - iant and true, For God and his kingdom take your stand; Go pub-lish the ti-dings, "Sal-va-tion is free," Till peace reigneth o-ver sea and land; Till hearts bowed in bit-ter-ness can smile thro' their weeping, Cease from their grief and glad-ly sing; Till ev-'ry knee shall bow before Him a - dor-ing, And ev-'ry heart shall own Him King.

3. Re - joice, and be glad, for the day draweth nigh, When kingdoms of earth shall own His sway; When truth, like a mantle, shall cov-er the earth, And sor-row and sighing flee a - way. O shout "hal-le - lu - jah" to Je-ho - vah Al-might-y! Let ev-'ry heart a trib-ute bring; Shout "hal-le-lu-jah," to the Sav-ior for-ev - er! Let all the earth with gladness ring.

COPYRIGHT, 1895, BY CHAS. H. GABRIEL.

NOTE.—"Bright Angels" should be sung by six little girls appropriately dressed, and arranged conspicuously upon the platform. Let six floral wreaths or crowns be prepared, each having one of the letters contained in the word "Angels" fixed upon it. Immediately after singing her stanza, let the appropriate crown be placed upon each girl's head. **All the school should sing in chorus.**

COPYRIGHT, 1891, BY CHAS. H. GABRIEL.

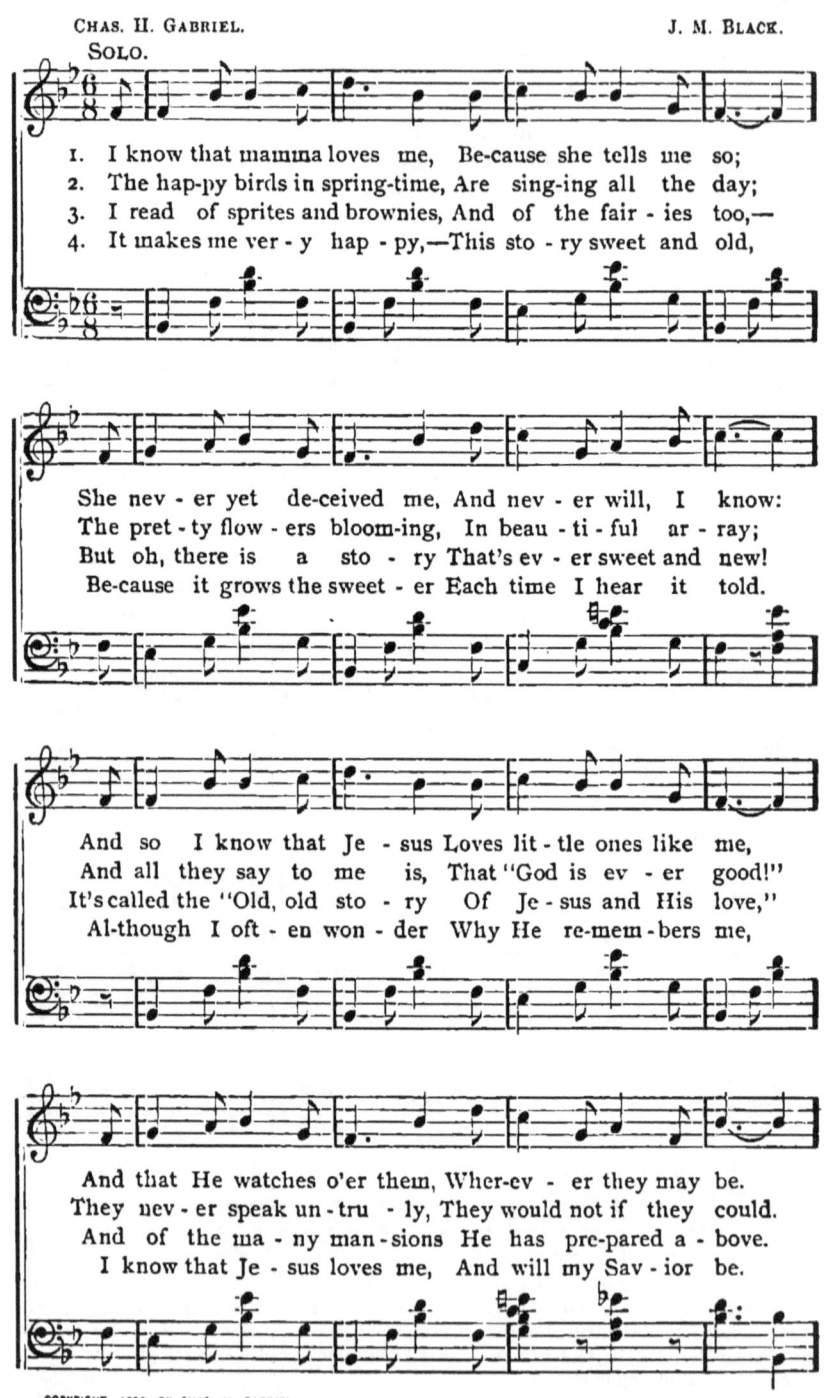

No. 91. HAPPY BEULAH LAND.

D. B. P.   D. B. PURINTON.

1. We are a lit-tle pil-grim band, Trav'ling on, trav-'ling on;
2. We are a lit-tle sol-dier band, Marching on, march-ing on;
3. We are a lit-tle work-ing band, Toil-ing on, toil-ing on;
4. We are a lit-tle Chris-tian band, Hop-ing on, hop-ing on;

We are a hap-py pil-grim band, Gai-ly trav-'ling on.
We are a fear-less, sol-dier band, Brave-ly march-ing on.
We are a bus-y work-ing band, Glad-ly toil-ing on.
We are an ear-nest Chris-tian band, Hop-ing, pray-ing on.

CHORUS.

On to the shores of the Beulah land, The happy land, the heav'nly land,

On to the shores of the Beu-lah land, The hap-py Beu-lah land.

BY PER. OF E. S. LORENZ, OWNER OF COPYRIGHT.

INDEX.

Title	No.
All hail the power	59
A loyal band	93
America	57
Anywhere with Jesus	23
A place and work for me	7
As a pilgrim band	38
As the Lord to Samuel	19
Battle hymn of missions	61
Be a golden sunbeam	53
Because He loves us so	47
Be not afraid	40
Bright angels	87
Bright Crowns	14
Carry the message	60
Children's battle song	75
Clean hands, pure hearts	86
Clinging to His promise	21
Come weal, come woe	40
Coronation	59
Dare to do right	9
Dare to think though	9
Do no sinful action	89
Do you fear the foe	31
Do you know the song	52
Eternal Father	61
Faith is the victory	18
Fierce is the tempest	78
For the beauty of the	83
Forward Christian wor	55
Forward ever forward	64
From the cross	58
Gather in the grain	49
Glorious news	60
Glory land	70
God is love	1
Go forth to work	82
Go gather in the	49
Happy Beulah land	91
Harvest fields	65
He leads and we follow	77
He loves them	44
He loves us so	88
Here am I	19
Hold me in Thy care	45
Holy, holy, holy	35
I have read of	22
I know that Mamma lo	88
In a midnight dungeon	87
In Christ is full	43
In the furrows of	27
Is there not a place for	63
I've found a friend	37
Jesus calls for faithful	54
Jesus is calling	26
Jesus leads the way	82
Jesus reigns	39
Jesus Shepherd lead us	33
Jesus the children's fri	85
Keep step ever	30
Lamb of God I look	45
Lead me all the way	25
Lead me Savior gently	25
Let the sunshine in	31
Let us rally, rally	28
Lifting as we climb	64
Little candles	92
Living in the sunshine	2
Lord dismiss us	67
Lo the harvest field	73
Loyal and true	50
Mansions in the Father	63
March along together	13
Marching on with glad	24
Marching home	38
Mizpah	69
My country 'tis of thee	57
Nearer every day	80
Nearer to Jesus	80
Now let us sing	8
O Calvary	36
O cross of grief	36
O'er hill and dale	77
O Jesus mighty Captain	75
Onward Christian work	55
Onward the foe to	71
Onward to glory	20
Onward up the highwa	76
O sing to the Savior	66
O soldier brave	32
Our Father who are	51
Out to the conflict	18
Praise the Lord	8
Rallying song	28
Ring all the bells	68
Room enough at Calvar	74
Room for all	74
Sailing, sailing	56
Sailing o'er the gospel	56
Scatter seed	43
Send the gospel message	4
Send the news	4
See the shining fields	65
Sing a song for Jesus	41
Sing the love of Jesus	5
Sing joyfully sing cheer	19
Singing speaking prayi	41
Shoulder to shoulder	12
Soldiers of Christ	32
Song of the Savior	79
Soldiers on life's battle	20
Steer toward the light	78
Sweetly sing the love	5
The child in the midst	62
The christian soldier	10
The glad good news	34
The light of the cross	58
The Lord bless thee and	67
The Lord watch betwee	69
The Lord's prayer	51
The sheaf and crown	66
The Sunday school arm	13
The sweet olden story	22
The unseen land	48
The work we love	3
Thee we praise	83
There is a happy land	29
There is a land	81
There is a land mine	48
There's work for all	6
Trust in God	72
Turn up your lamp	11
Victory	71
Victory by and by	42
We are but little candl	92
We are little soldiers	90
We are little pilgrims	91
We are marching	16
We are marching on	24
We are marching onwa	42
We are willing workers	15
We come together	3
We love to sing	47
We love to sing of Jesus	85
We're a happy band	16
We're soldiers in the	10
We're little christian	93
We're on our way	70
What a blessed salvatio	27
When Jesus was asked	62
When the roll is called	84
When His salvation	44
When skies are blue	17
When the harvest wave	7
When the trumpet of	84
Whether with the few	72
Whispered by the even	1
While there's a little	50
Who will gather	73
Willing workers	15
Will you do what you	46
With an everlasting lov	34
Work for all	6
Would you gain the	30

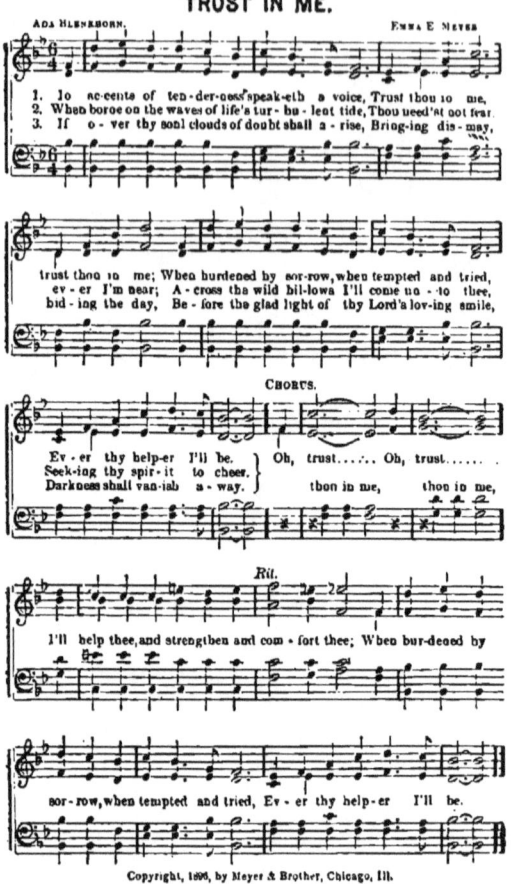

www.ingramcontent.com/pod-product-compliance
Lightning Source LLC
Chambersburg PA
CBHW031120160426
43192CB00008B/1061